This book is dedicated to all of the people, places and creatures I have loved.

My Dad Died
Reflections of a Child

Written By Lea M. Gorgulu Webb

Illustrated By H. Meral Tolunay

© 2012 Lea M. Gorgulu Webb

My name is Jasmin. I live with my mom and my brother.
We lived with my dad, too, until he got very sick. He went to the hospital, and they could not make him better. He died.
Now, it is just me and my mom and my brother.

I miss my dad, and I want things to be the way they were, before he became sick.

I miss the things I remember about everyday,
like how my dad laughed when I put on funny costumes
and did funny dances...

and how he read books to me...
and EVERYDAY he told me he loved me.
I loved my dad more than all the fish in the seas!

Missing someone is the most terrible feeling.
When I am sad and missing my dad,
it feels like
I have a big hole in my heart.
Sometimes, I cry or want to cry.
Sometimes, I feel like I cannot talk,
or all I will do is cry.
Other times, I just feel like I don't have
any energy at all. My head even feels heavy,
like I can't hold it up, when I'm sad.

I know my mom feels sad like this a lot. She looked very sick after daddy died. It was scary. I was scared that she might get sick and die, too. Then, she cried a lot. Almost all the time, I think.

Now, she only cries sometimes. If I ask her why, she says, "Because I miss daddy." She hugs me sometimes and says that it is okay to cry and I don't need to worry about her... but I do. I don't want her to be sad.

I talked to her about how my tears make me feel better: like cold water on a burnt finger, or washing off a boo boo. It's important for the tears to flow and the sadness to come out. One day, I saw mom cry a lot. I told her, "Wow! You should feel much better!" She laughed, even though she had tears on her face. The same thing happens to me when I cry; I feel a little better. Then, I can do something else.

My mom exercises to help her feel
happier, too. I can tell she feels
better after getting some exercise.
It seems like the way I feel after
playing and running.
I like to have fun with my mom when
she exercises.
We feel strong and energized after a
good work out!

Exercising and playing were hard after daddy died. I was just a little kid, then. (Now, I am a big kid.) I loved to play and run and ride my bike. (Bike riding is my favorite thing in the world. To me it is always exciting and electric!)

After daddy died, though, when I played or rode my bike, I felt bad about myself. I thought, "Shouldn't I just be sad? Am I bad for laughing and playing?" I felt guilty for having fun without him or for being happy after he died.

I know that daddy would want me to have as much fun as possible, because he was fun. It was hard not to feel bad about playing. So, I told my mom one day that I felt guilty. We decided to practice! We went to the park to think about daddy, while having fun. We ran and chased and rolled down the hills.

Daddy loved to watch me roll down hills. If I remember how he loved to have fun, it is easier to stop feeling guilty. Now, if I feel guilty, I imagine the sound of him laughing.

I also love to read (like my dad).
Some of my favorite books have kids with dads in them.
Reading them can make me feel sad and jealous.
When I am reading, I remember daddy, and sometimes I imagine that he
is still alive. I pretend that I am reading to him.
I was learning to read when he died. Once, after I became a strong reader,
I tried reading ALL of my books - out loud - to make him
magically come back.
Sadly, it didn't work. Reading still made me feel proud of myself, and I
know that daddy would have been proud of me, too.

When daddy first died, I was often very jealous of other families: jealous of families with a daddy. When I felt jealous, I began to feel a little angry, too, even though nobody did anything. My mom and brother shared the same feelings with me and we talked about it. We talked about how different every family is. Everyone has different people to love and miss.

My grandparents can come and see me in the school play, while others don't have grandparents. I have aunts and uncles, while others don't. The truth is that I am jealous because I like what the other person has: a dad. This jealous feeling starts to go away when I realize that I'm sad that I don't have my dad. Thank goodness, I have some really good friends, and a couple have dads that treat me the way my dad would have. It is really nice. I'm glad we have these good friends.

I learned that I was feeling jealous from talking to my mom and Jon. Talking to them about how I feel is a little easier than talking to other people. They have a lot of the same feelings (but not all). Talking to friends or teachers can be really hard.

It is hard to tell people how you feel, when you don't know yourself. Sometimes it makes me tired of the questions. Jon agrees with me about this. We don't know how to explain that we are very sad and mad, and maybe we don't want to talk about it with everyone.

When my friends ask me if my dad is really dead, I tell them, "yes."
My brother, though, doesn't like for anyone to talk about it. It makes him really frustrated and angry. He thinks he is angry at the person who asks, but I know he, like me, is not really angry at the person asking the question.
We are just frustrated and angry.
We want our dad back!
We can't always explain how jealous or sad we are or that we feel like crying.
Sometimes we want to talk, and sometimes we don't!
The person who asks is probably trying to be nice, and doesn't realize what kind of storm we have inside.

We learned some ways to answer questions from our "support group." After daddy died, we went to meetings with some other kids and moms and dads who had also lost someone important. Mom said these are "support groups." (I don't really know why they are called that. No one there ever picks me up or helps me walk. Isn't that what support means?) It is a fun place to go, though. All of my friends there are like me. I never thought there would be so many kids like me — with a parent who died. At our group meetings, we made lots of things, like special pictures about the people who died and memory boxes to keep our memories in. We played and sang and even danced. It was easier to talk there, where we were all feeling some of the same strong things.

Drawing has been an important thing for me. I have a journal I take with me most days. When a grown up or a kid says something that makes me sad about daddy, I draw a picture or write a note. I like to do this more than talking. After I draw some, I usually feel better. My heart feels more like a butterfly than a rock, again. It is kind of like magic. I love to draw my dad and my family and everyone together.

I gave a journal to my uncle, too, and I gave some of the pictures I drew to my grandparents. We have a lot of people in our family who are all sad about daddy dying. Daddy's brothers and sisters miss him very much. He was their big brother. They felt special when he was around, because he loved his little brothers and sisters. Now, they don't have him. They are a lot like me. They miss him; we all look like him, and we all like to play.

That makes me happy, because it is like I still have daddy to hug. I still feel loved from my dad, even if it is someone else hugging me. And since I look like daddy, when people see me, they see a little bit of him. Hugging me is like hugging daddy - for them.
They can't hug the mirror, after all!

I asked my nice uncles to be my new dad. They said, they love me, but they are my uncles. "We can be special friends, but we can't be your dad." Mommy and I talked about it and decided that they need to be the uncles in our family. Aunts and uncles and grandparents are very special people. Mine are lots of fun and sometimes give me presents that my mom won't give me: like noisy toys or balls that might break something in the house. Also, without aunts and uncles, there are no cousins. Cousins are some of my best friends. So, I'll let them be who they are, and I will be me, and we will keep having fun and loving each other like this.

My family is different without daddy. I will always miss him. Days pass, and I realize that I am growing up and changing and learning. I used to be very afraid I would forget him, but I'm not so afraid of that anymore. Everyday, I remember him many times. Remembering him sometimes makes me sad, but, in a way, it also makes me feel good.

Made in the USA
Middletown, DE
31 January 2016